Gift of the
Concordia Faculty Women

ME and
EINSTEIN

For Michael

ME and EINSTEIN

Breaking through the Reading Barrier

by

ROSE BLUE

Illustrated by

Peggy Luks

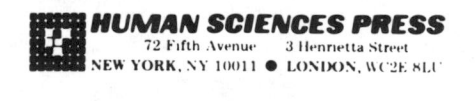
HUMAN SCIENCES PRESS
72 Fifth Avenue   3 Henrietta Street
NEW YORK, NY 10011 ● LONDON, WC2E 8LU

Library of Congress Catalog Number 79-11387
ISBN: 0-87705-388-X

Copyright © 1979 by
Human Sciences Press, 72 Fifth Avenue, New York, N.Y. 10011

Printed in the United States of America

9   9 8 7 6 5 4 3 2 1

Library of Congress Cataloging in Publication Data

Blue, Rose.
    Me and Einstein.

    SUMMARY: Having tried for years to hide the fact that
he can't read, a nine-year-old boy finally discovers the reason for his problem.
    [1.   Reading—Fiction. 2.   Dyslexia—Fiction] I. Title.
PZ7.B6248Ei   [Fic]   79-11387
ISBN 0-87705-388-X

Chapter One

SUNLIGHT FILLED the yard and glistened on the colorful umbrellas. The lawn looked shiny and magical. It had the feel of a small, private carnival. There was even a tent that Dad had set up in case it rained.

The wind blowing the streamers made a soft tinkling sound. A banner reading Happy Birthday Aunt Lillian was strung across the grass. Bobby knew what the words on the banner said. He remembered his Dad speaking the words the day they had decorated the lawn.

The August Saturday was perfect. Bobby sat near Aunt Lillian, nibbling potato chips as the aroma of his Dad's barbecuing drifted through the air. His folks were giving a small lunch party for Aunt Lillian. There would be other parties for her during the weekend. But Bobby was glad he had helped make her birthday happy.

His parents said Aunt Lillian was fifty years old. That sounded pretty old but his aunt seemed young. She was always laughing and fun to have around and she never seemed to say the wrong thing to a kid like other grownups did. She always brought a present. Today she had brought a present for Bobby, even though it was her birthday. Bobby didn't open it because his aunt hadn't opened her presents yet. But he hoped that maybe it was a football.

Sprint walked up and laid his cheek on Bobby's knee. Bobby didn't think potato chips were good for dogs but he gave him one anyway. Sprint curled up near Bobby, then he began barking.

"I think someone's outside," Mom said. "Would you see who's there Bobby?"

"Sure Mom."

Bobby walked out of the backyard, Sprint following after him. The postman was outside the door.

"Hi Bobby," he said. He reached down, petted Sprint, then handed Bobby a letter.

"That's all the mail today," he said.

"Thanks Mr. Crawford."

Bobby looked at the envelope. It was from his sister Annette. He could tell from the Snoopy stationery. Annette loved Snoopy. The Charlie Brown characters were all over her room. Annette had gone to scout camp for the month of August. Lots of kids did. But Bobby stayed home. He hated meeting new people and he always felt far behind the other kids at sports.

Bobby walked back to the party.

"Who was that?" Dad asked.

"Mr. Crawford."

"Oh any mail today?"

"Only one letter," Bobby said. "From Annette."

"Hey great," Mom said. "It's the first letter we got from her since she went to camp."

Uncle John, Cousin Lucy, Cousin Claire and Aunt Sylvia seemed to form a chorus. "Open it," they said.

"Read it."

"Read it Bobby."

"We'd love to hear how Annette is doing."

"Read it Bobby, read it Bobby."

Bobby opened the letter slowly. He took it from the envelope and unfolded it. Then he reached down, petted Sprint and whispered into the dog's ear. No one else heard the words "run Sprint." Bobby had taken a lot of time with his pet. Sprint was well trained. He ran

quickly toward the open outside gate. Bobby dropped the letter to the grass and ran after Sprint.

He ran out the gate and down the street. It was a neat trick. It had worked. He didn't have to stand there, like an idiot, in front of his aunts, uncles and cousins, trying to figure out the words of a letter. He didn't have to stand there ashamed and embarrassed before his family, while they learned that he couldn't read. His secret was still safe. Nine years old and he couldn't read. How much longer would he have to think up tricks? New ways to fool everybody?

He ran on down the street, Sprint right with him. Running from his family, running from the party, running from the truth. Then he stopped as the tooting of a car horn sounded loudly and steadily at the curb beside him.

"Hey Bobby," Mr. Morrison called. "How about a lift to the beach?"

Bobby walked over to the car. "Thanks, but we've got company."

"We won't be long. Just going for a swim. We're having some people over in an hour."

Bobby thought of Aunt Lillian. She might think it was funny if he stayed away from her party for too long. Then he thought of the letter. Nobody caught on. He was pretty sure. Still, he didn't feel like going back and facing everyone. Not just yet.

"Sure Mr. Morrison," he said as he and Sprint climbed into the back of the station wagon.

Bobby figured the Morrisons had invited him along because they missed Joe. Kind of like renting a kid for a little while. But Bobby didn't mind. He liked the Morrisons even if he wasn't too crazy about Joe.

"Have you heard from Annette?" Mrs. Morrison asked.

"We got a letter from her this morning."

"Is she enjoying camp?"

"I guess so," Bobby said.

"We left before the postman came," Mrs. Morrison said. "Maybe there'll be a letter when we get back."

"Sure there will Mrs. Morrison."

"We really do miss our boy," Mrs. Morrison said. "Our only child and he's never been away before." She laughed. "I must sound silly."

"No. You sound like a mom."

Mrs. Morrison turned and smiled. "I guess I do. We were surprised you didn't go to scout camp."

"I didn't feel like it. And I'm training Sprint."

"You sure are doing great with that dog," Mr. Morrison said. "You really adopted him. But won't you miss him when the Grants get home?"

"Boy would I. But maybe I won't have to. You know the Grants left Sprint with us when they went to the city in June. Mr. Grant is trying out a new job and their apartment is small. If Mr. Grant gets to keep his job I'll get to keep Sprint."

"Well I hope everything works out for you and the Grants," Mr. Morrison said. He slowed down and pointed to a sprawling old house with a sign on the lawn.

"Look there, Bobby," he said. "That's Doctor Adamson's place. He's the best veterinarian in town. Lives and works there. Remember that in case Sprint ever gets sick or anything. Doctor Adamson will see you anytime."

Bobby studied the house so that he would recognize it again. The sign probably had Dr. Adamson's name on it. But studying the house was easier for Bobby than trying to make out the name. He counted the blocks as Mr. Morrison drove. The veterinarian was

four blocks from the beach entrance parking lot. Bobby made a careful mental note of that. You never know when Sprint might need a doctor.

Mr. Morrison pulled into the lot. Everyone left the station wagon and walked to the lockers.

"We'll just take a little swim," Mrs. Morrison said. "There's a brand new pair of Joe's trunks in the locker. They should fit you."

"I'd like to take Sprint for a little walk on the beach," Bobby said after they changed their clothes.

"Okay," Mrs. Morrison said. "But don't wander off for too long. We have to get back."

"I won't."

"We'll meet you right here in front of the lifeguard's stand."

Bobby ran along the shore, Sprint beside him. That was about all he could do in sports, he thought. Running, football and swimming. Things that didn't call for catching small things. He was terrible at baseball. His hands just never could grab a baseball and hold it.

Bobby looked back. He could still see the lifeguard stand. He didn't want to go too much farther. He might get lost. He sat down near the shore. "Sit Sprint," he said, patting the sand.

Bobby put his arm around Sprint's neck and looked out at the ocean. The thought of the letter from Annette kept coming back to him. He had the same trouble at his ninth birthday party in May. People put birthday cards inside his presents and when he opened the gifts he couldn't tell who they were from. He pretended to read the cards, smiled and said, "Gee thanks. This is great." Then whoever had given the gift would say, "Glad you like it." He could tell who gave some gifts by their wrappings. Joe's birthday was the week before and Bobby recognized the paper and ribbons on some of the gifts. That way he could say, "thanks Martha," or "that's great Les," while he looked at the card. He had faked that one through okay.

When Bobby was little everyone thought his baby talk was cute. Then in kindergarten he did okay. Bobby remembered back to the Simon Says games in first grade. That and the Hokey Pokey and Looby Loo. You were supposed to put your right hand in, left hand out and stuff, and Bobby could never get right and left straight. His teacher didn't seem to take it too seriously though.

Then when everyone learned to read, Bobby had a terrible time. He couldn't get the letters straight. He couldn't see the words the way everyone else saw them. But Bobby was smart. And his memory was great. He would remember the story word for word when the teacher read it. He would study the pictures. Then when he was called on he pretended to read the story. He had faked it then, and for the most part, he was still faking it. In school, and at parties. But

for how long? Bobby picked up a stick that had washed up on shore. He tried to write his name in the sand. It came out ꓭoddy. He looked up and saw the Morrisons waving to him. He threw the stick into the shallow water, far across the shore line. Together he and Sprint swam quickly toward the stick and the lifeguard stand.

When Bobby got back Aunt Lillian greated him warmly. "I missed my nephew," she said. "Where have you been?"

"I met the Morrisons. They took me for a swim. I didn't mean to be gone long."

"You weren't. You're back in plenty of time for eating, cake cutting and present opening."

Bobby laughed and sat with his aunt. "That's good," he said.

Aunt Lillian looked at the gaily decorated table. The cake was out now. "The cake is beautiful," she said. She smiled. "Happy Birthday Aunt Lillian," she said. "Well I'm glad they didn't put any age on it."

"Don't be silly, Aunt Lillian," Bobby said. "You'll never even act old."

Aunt Lillian put her arm around him. "My Bobby always had a silver tongue."

Bobby looked around the party table. He spotted the Snoopy letter. It lay near the decorated cake, near all the birthday cards. Near all the word-filled things he couldn't make out. He snuggled closer to Aunt Lillian as the words "read it Bobby," "read it," "read it," kept echoing back to him through the soft summer breeze.

Chapter Two

AS THE SUMMER drew to a close Bobby became more and more upset. August had been a real vacation time for him. It was as though he had found a safe snug harbor on a far away island. His folks were at work all day. There was nobody to shove books at him, to try to get him to read, to make him wish he lived somewhere else, with some other family.

Sometimes he wished he lived with Mrs. Allan, who stayed in the house while his mom was at work. She cooked delicious dishes, and always called him over, saying, "here Bobby taste." She looked after him, never bothered him, and when she dusted she would laugh and say, "my goodness look at all these books. A person would think you lived in a bookstore."

It was so safe and simple just being with Mrs. Allan and Sprint. It was like being with Aunt Lillian. Warm and cozy with nobody expecting you to do anything special before they could love you. Many times Bobby felt that his parents would care for him only when he learned to do all the things they felt their nine year old son should do. Many times he felt that those book-lined walls were closing in on him, squeezing the breath from his lungs and choking him.

During August he could sit in the yard with Sprint, walk around the block, and hang around the kitchen as the delicious smells of Mrs. Allan's cooking made him feel as though he were in a real home. When everyone was around Bobby felt like he was an outsider who everyone wished would go away. His father was an editor, his mother was a librarian, and Annette at twelve years old was well

into reading her way through every book in the house. When everyone was home, Bobby felt out of place, unnecessary and dumb.

Now the summer was ending, Annette would be home and school would begin. He would have to go from a school room where he was supposed to read to a home where he was supposed to read. There would be no relief. No more safe harbor. No more escape. The days of Bobby, Mrs. Allan and Sprint would soon be over.

When the Labor Day holiday arrived Bobby began to feel the panic shooting through him. The only comfort through the far too fast moving weekend was the phone call from the Grants. Bobby answered the telephone on that Sunday.

"Bobby," Mr. Grant said. "I'm getting a promotion and keeping my job in the city."

"That's great Mr. Grant," Bobby said.

"We're putting the house up for sale and keeping our city apartment. How would you like to keep Sprint?"

Bobby let a wild war whoop. "Boy would I ever," he said loudly.

His parents came running in.

"Mr. Grant is getting a good job. He wants me to keep Sprint. Can I? Can I?"

His parents laughed. "Sure, always room for one more," his mother said.

"Let me talk to Jim Grant a minute." Dad said. "I'd like to hear about the job."

Bobby handed the phone to his Dad and ran to his room. He sat on the floor, leaned against the wall and pulled Sprint to him. He rubbed the dog's long hair. "You're going to stay here with me Sprint," he said. "We're going to be together." He petted Sprint slowly. "But we won't be together all the time anymore," he said sadly. "School starts Tuesday, Sprint, and I'm scared."

The beginning of the new school year was far worse than Bobby had feared. Teachers had always liked Bobby. He had been a cute little kid with black curly hair and big dark eyes. When he was young he mixed up words sometimes, and spoke in baby talk. Grownups used to think it was funny. He had stopped doing that, but he was still a cute kid to lots of grownups.

Back in first and second grade he did fine. Nobody seemed to catch on to the trouble he had putting words together. He wasn't sure he fooled his third grade teacher though. Miss Scott liked him and she was really nice. Bobby still memorized the words of stories he heard read aloud. He still managed to pretend he was reading the stories aloud. But it got harder to do in third grade. When he missed a word or two, Miss Scott would correct him, but she never made a big thing out of it. She never pushed or pressed him to read either. Bobby wasn't sure how much Miss Scott really knew.

Now, as the new term began, Bobby was sure of one thing. He wasn't going to fool Mrs. Roth. She was wise to him and she was tough. She didn't seem to care about his curly hair or big dark eyes either. She didn't like his reading. She was fooled about one thing though. She didn't really know how much of his reading he had learned by memory.

Still, fourth grade work was a lot harder than third. He made many more mistakes. And Mrs. Roth wasn't happy with him. She thought he was goofing off. She thought fourth grade was serious stuff. And she meant business. The autumn leaves had barely begun to turn when she dragged Bobby's parents up to school to see her.

There was a parent conference night after the first few weeks of school. All the other kids got letters run off on a machine. Bobby got a handwritten note clipped to the notice. When his folks got home from work they read the letters.

"The notice is for a conference next Wednesday," Dad said. "And there's a special note to us."

Mom took the note and read it aloud.

Dear Mr. and Mrs. Dawson,

Please note that the first parent conference night will be held next Wednesday. We feel that meetings early in the term help to solve problems that appear.

I am most anxious to see you both. If for any reason you cannot attend this meeting, please let me know and I will arrange another night.

Yours truly,

Mrs. Roth

Dad looked at Bobby. "Sounds serious," he said. "Did you get into any trouble?"

"No, Dad, I didn't do anything wrong."

"Well this note means something," Mom said. "We'll find out soon enough."

Bobby went to the conference with his folks. He sat in back of the room while Mrs. Roth sat up front at her desk talking with his parents. Mr. and Mrs. Dawson sat on chairs near the side of Mrs. Roth's desk.

Other parents waited in back of the room. One or two kids in class sat there, too, fidgeting nervously. They must have gotten special letters, just like he did. Steve and Charlie hardly ever behaved in class. It wasn't hard to figure why they were there.

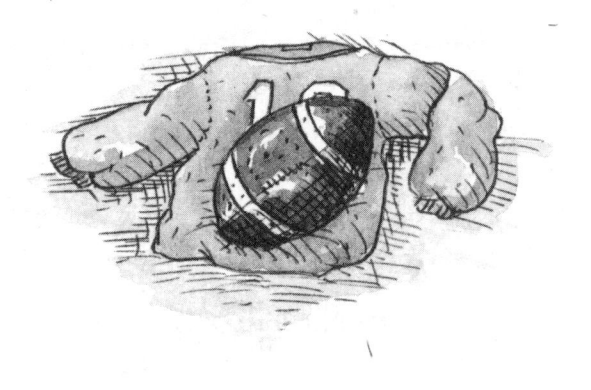

Bobby got up and walked around the side of the room. He acted as though he was looking at the new bulletin boards on the wall. But he was listening hard, trying to hear what Mrs. Roth was telling his parents. He caught snatches of the conversation. "He likes math. Uses the calculator. Likes art. Football. That sweater he wears all the time. But reading is the major problem." Their voices grew too low for him to hear for awhile. Then he caught some more of Mrs. Roth's words. He heard her say, "he won't try. If he would only do his work—" And, "maybe he's trying to rebel. Sometimes at this age."

Bobby thought he knew what the word rebel meant. He had heard it used on T. V. shows. It meant not listening to the people you were supposed to listen to. Not following the rules. But if rules meant reading the way other nine year olds did, he just couldn't obey Mrs. Roth.

After the meeting nobody really spoke to Bobby about it. Mr. and Mrs. Dawson talked together in low tones. They would quit talking when he walked into the room. It was as though they were trying to decide what to say to him. How to solve what Mrs. Roth called "the problem." Only the problem wasn't reading. The problem was him.

Then, that weekend the house exploded. It was like a slow burning firecracker fuse that suddenly blew. Bobby had been out running with Sprint and tossing the football Aunt Lillian had given him. He was wearing his favorite sweater against the Saturday morning autumn breeze. Bobby loved that sweatshirt. It had the number ten across the back. That was the number of Bobby Dryfuss, the quarterback of the Western Stars. The sweater made Bobby feel important. Bobby Dryfuss had the same first name as he did, and even the same last initial. Someday, when Bobby's writing was better, he would send a letter to Bobby Dryfuss letting him know how much he admired him, and how he loved football too.

When Bobby got back his parents were sitting in the living room.

"Been out with Sprint again, Bobby?" Mr. Dawson asked. "What are you doing this afternoon?"

Bobby shrugged. "Watching the game, I guess. The Stars are playing."

"Any homework?" Mom asked. "When are you fitting that in?"

"I'll do it after the game."

"Football," Mom said loudly. "Running and football. Don't you ever do anything else?" Her words came thick and fast, like heavily falling snowflakes in a sudden storm. "And that sweater. Lately you don't take it off long enough to get it laundered."

Bobby pulled the sweater more tightly to him. "I like it," he said.

"Mrs. Roth said you even wore it to assembly," Dad said. "She also told us you do nothing but use your calculator and do art work. She's very worried about your reading."

Bobby looked around at the room. He felt stifled by the voices of his parents, by the books filling the room, by the words all around

him. "Mrs. Roth is a pain," he yelled loudly, as he ran up the stairs to his room holding the football.

His parents followed quickly behind him. "Now look Bobby," Mr. Dawson said. "We do have to talk."

Bobby had enough talk for one day. It seemed to him that all this talk only meant more trouble with words.

"Could we talk later?" he said. "I'm kind of busy now."

"Busy with what?" his mother yelled sarcastically. "That calculator of yours? The football game? Running with your dog? That's all you do. Except drawing pictures all the time. Just look at these walls." She waved her hand around the room. "Covered with silly drawings."

"What's all the noise about?" Annette said. "I was reading in my room and I heard yelling."

Bobby looked at his sister. She stood calmly in the doorway, tall and slim, her long blonde hair neatly brushed, wearing a clean quilted robe, holding a book in her hand. Suddenly he hated her. He hated them all. "You don't yell at her," he shrieked. "You don't say a word about her walls. All messed up with those dumb Snoopy posters. You just pick on me."

His father walked up to him and put a hand on his shoulder. He shrugged his father's hand off and kept shrieking, "Get out, get out all of you. Get out and leave me alone."

He sat on his bed and turned his face to the wall. He lay there, clutching Aunt Lillian's football to his sweatshirt, rocking from one side of the bed to the other, as everyone left him, just as he had asked, all, all alone.

Chapter Three

THE NEXT DAYS were one long, lonesome sadness for Bobby. He went from home to school to home, feeling as though he didn't really belong in either place. Mrs. Roth was annoyed with him at school and his parents were upset with him at home. There was no relief, no change from the day to day routine, and each day was filled with a heavy gloom.

Bobby tried to keep to himself in school, to avoid being called on to read or to answer questions. But Mrs. Roth just seemed to push and press all the time.

One day Mrs. Roth was working on a Social Studies unit. Most of the time the class worked from the same textbooks. Bobby had managed to figure out enough of their regular books to half way get by. But this time Mrs. Roth gave out some special material. She had taken some pages that came inside a weekly magazine, stapled them together, and made her own little book. Bobby had never seen this book before and he was in trouble.

There were pictures of flags in the book and Bobby figured out that Mrs. Roth was going to teach about the flags of other countries. Bobby knew most of the flags by looking at the pictures, but there were one or two he didn't recognize. Bobby sat clenching his fists under the desk, hoping that Mrs. Roth would call on him for one of the flags he knew. He could have answered France, Switzerland, England, but Mrs. Roth called on the other kids for those countries. Bobby stared at the next picture. He shut his eyes, opened them and stared hard again. He had seen that flag somewhere before, but he couldn't place it. Then, like a clap of thunder on a still, sleepy night,

Mrs. Roth's voice was booming his name.

"Bobby, the next answer please."

Bobby sat, looking at the page, staring and staring.

"Bobby," Mrs. Roth said irritably. "Bobby, I called your name. You are not answering. To what country does that flag belong?"

Bobby kept staring at the page, not lifting his head, trying to remember the flag.

"Bobby," Mrs. Roth said evenly. "The name of the country is written right under the flag."

"Yeah, Bobby, can't you read?"

Bobby turned.

That voice belonged to Maurice. Wise guy, snooty Maurice, always wearing a white shirt to assembly, always putting people down, always getting the right answers.

"Bobby baby can't read," he said in a sing song voice.

Bobby turned to Maurice. "I know the answer," he said cooly. "This flag is from Mars." He ripped the page out of the book loudly, then he shaped it into a rocket and aimed it straight at Maurice's smart mouth. "And here it is coming right at you."

The kids began laughing, and the classroom became bedlam. Maurice ducked as the rocket flew at him. Bobby got out of his seat and walked up to Maurice. He lifted him half way out of his seat by that white shirt of his.

"Sure I can read," he said. "I can read you. Right there, written all over your face, it says chicken."

Maurice did look scared. He hadn't expected this. And he wasn't used to fighting.

Bobby knocked Maurice from his chair. In a minute the two boys were rolling all over the classroom floor, punching and dodging punches. The kids were out of their seats, running around the room, watching the fight.

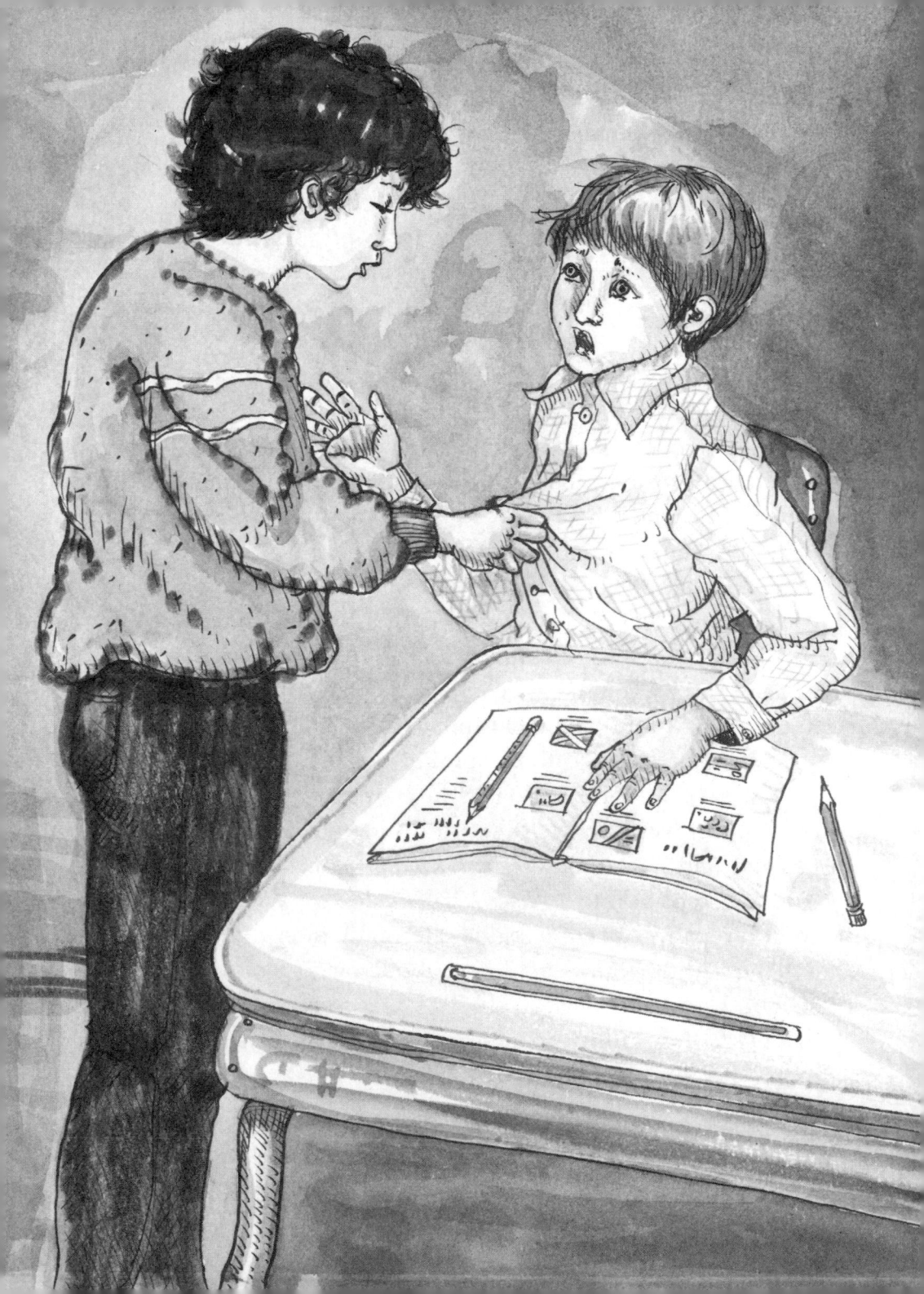

Mrs. Roth stood in front of the room, banging a heavy ruler loudly against her desk.

"I want order now," she said loudly and clearly. "Anyone not in their seats in a minute will be reported to the principal." Most of the kids sat down. Maurice broke free and went to his seat. Bobby was about to sit down when Steven and Charlie walked up to him, lifted him off the floor, and held him between them. They yelled "three cheers for Bobby the champ."

Then they shouted rah, rah, rah, three times, as some of the kids followed their lead. Mrs. Roth rapped for order once again. The class grew quiet. Steve and Charlie laughed and put Bobby down.

"I'll want to see you after school today Bobby," she said. "Along with Steven and Charlie."

Bobby went back to his seat. He couldn't believe what he had done. He had never behaved that way in school before. Not ever. But he didn't feel the least bit sorry or ashamed. In fact, he felt glad, and good, and in a strange way proud of himself. He was with Charlie and Steven. He was a bad kid. That's the way the other kids in the class would begin to think of him. And that was okay. It was a lot better to be bad than dumb.

Mrs. Roth's scolding floated high above Bobby, like the distant roar of an overhead jet. She said things like "I'll be calling your parents," and "I won't have this kind of behavior in my classroom." And she kept asking "why? What made you act this way?" Bobby couldn't answer her questions. He really didn't know the answers and he didn't really care. Not about his reasons for fighting in school. Not about Mrs. Roth. The kids were cheering him instead of putting him down or laughing at him, and that was what mattered.

When he got home Mrs. Allan was in the kitchen. She said, "You're a little late today Bobby. Did you have a good day at school?"

He said "fine Mrs. Allan," and tasted some soup that she held out to him on a big wooden stirring spoon. He went out to walk Sprint, then he came back and hung around the front yard. His mother came home soon afterwards, "Hi Bobby," she said. "How'd school go today?"

He held his breath. "Okay I guess," he said, trying to sound calm. Mrs. Allan hadn't said anything, and Mom was cool, so he guessed that Mrs. Roth hadn't called.

Not yet anyway.

His mom leaned against the fence. "Beautiful day," she said. "Real Indian summer."

Bobby looked up the block. Charlie and Steven were riding their bicycles, heading right for his house. They braked right near the curb.

"Hey Bobby," Steve said excitedly. "We've been riding around. There's an ice cream truck parked a few blocks away on Elmhurst Street."

"Yeah," Charlie said. "The back door's open and nobody's in it. We don't know where the ice cream man is."

"Come on Bobby," Steve said. "Let's go get ourselves some treats."

Bobby was amazed. His mom was right next to him and those guys were acting like she wasn't even there. They didn't care about moms, parents, or any other grownups.

"Come on," Steve said impatiently. "We'll miss out."

Bobby hopped on the handlebars and Steve raced off, with

Charlie beside him. "Bobby, come back," his mom called as she ran after him. "Bobby, get back here." She kept running and calling, but she could never out run Steve's bike and soon the sound of her voice grew dimmer and faded away.

Bobby knew it was wrong, going off like that, taking something that didn't belong to him. But Steve and Charlie had come to call for him. They had come over to his house. He was one of them. He belonged some place. And he felt very, very important.

When they got to the truck, it was still open and empty. Charlie reached into the back of the truck when the ice cream man, wearing his uniform, walked out of a nearby house.

"Hey Charlie" Steve yelled. "The ice cream man is coming. Let's get out of here."

Charlie leaped onto his bike, and Steve took off, Bobby riding the handlebars. Bobby looked back, as the ice cream man stood, shaking his fist and yelling, "you rotten kids. I'll get you yet."

When they got far enough away from where the truck was parked, Steve asked Bobby if he wanted to go home. A sudden fear hit Bobby. He didn't want to face his folks right now.

"I don't feel like going home yet," he said coolly. "I think I'll just hang around awhile." He looked around and saw the schoolyard up the street. He didn't know where Steve or Charlie lived, or how to get home from wherever they dropped him. He couldn't read the street signs well, but he knew his way home from school. "Drop me here," he said calmly. "I'll go home later."

He stood alone in the empty schoolyard, afraid to go home. By now his Dad would be back from work, Mom would have told him about Charlie and Steve, and most likely Mrs. Roth had called. He picked up a magic marker lying on the concrete, bent down on one knee, and wrote his name on the top step of the schoolyard. He leaned closer and read what he had written. Again it came out ꟼoddy. He sighed and tossed away the used, nearly dried up marker. He turned and began walking down the steps. "Bobby," his dad called. "Bobby get over here."

Dad was sitting in his car, parked at the curb, the motor running, honking his horn loudly. Mom was beside him. There was no running away from it. Bobby sighed and walked slowly to the car. He got in and his father drove off.

"We've been riding around looking all over for you," Mom said shakily. "I didn't have the car today until Dad came home."

"Do you know what you've done, Bobby?" Dad said evenly. "How you've upset your mother? And that's for openers. Running off to take things from an ice cream truck. You do understand that's stealing." His father's voice rose on the last word, making it sound really serious, the way the minister did in church.

"We didn't take anything. The ice cream man was near the truck when we got there. And anyway I wasn't going to take anything. I just figured to hang around, watching Charlie and Steve."

"And you think that makes it all right? Don't you know that's just as wrong as stealing? And by the way, Mrs. Roth called about your performance in school today. You seem to be getting into trouble every which way."

Bobby looked out the car window. The sun was setting above the roof of the houses. The sky looked calm and peaceful. Mom was terribly upset and worried, Dad was furious, and Bobby was enjoying the ride. He was being noticed for a change, not because he was dumb, not because he couldn't read, but because he was getting into trouble. His folks were caring about him. They were looking at him as though he was a real person, talking to him as though he was really there. Being bad had never felt so good.

Early next morning Bobby's parents were at school. This time Mrs. Roth met the Dawsons in the principal's office. This time

Bobby had to sit outside, on a hard wooden bench, the curtained door to the principal's office shut to him. And this time when Mrs. Roth greeted his parents, her face looked grim.

Bobby didn't feel as good about being bad as he had yesterday. Still he was being noticed. His parents were here. The principal was talking with them. His teacher had come in early, and everyone was making this big fuss over him. Over Bobby Dawson. Bobby felt excited and a little scared at the same time. Then the door to the principal's office opened.

"Come in Bobby," Mrs. Lehman said.

Bobby walked in and sat down. He felt kind of important, getting inside the principal's office.

"We're going to put you in a different class, Bobby," Mrs. Lehman said. "We've decided that you might do better in school that way."

Boy, Bobby thought, he was getting out of that pesty Mrs. Roth's class. That was terrific. He wouldn't have to look at her sour face anymore or listen to her nagging. Maybe they were taking him out of Mrs. Roth's class because she was mean to him. Maybe the new teacher would be nice, like Miss Scott last year.

"Who will my new teacher be?" he asked.

"You will be going to Miss Martin's class," Mrs. Lehman said.

"What class is that? I don't know Miss Martin."

"It's a special education class," Mrs. Roth said.

Bobby was surprised, but pleased. They were putting him in a special class, treating him as though he were special. Maybe it was because they were sorry about the nasty way Mrs. Roth had treated him.

Later, when Bobby thought about the new class, he began to feel more frightened and worried. Mrs. Roth's class was rough, but at least he knew what he was dealing with. He would miss Charlie and Steve, too. Still, he told himself, he would stay buddies with them. They shared exciting secrets, and he had acted really cool when they called for him to sneak ice cream from the truck. He was one of them now.

Funny, he would miss the other kids too. Even the ones he couldn't stand, like Maurice. He became more uneasy and puzzled. What did special education class mean? And if they figured he was bad why were they putting him in a special class? After dinner Bobby asked his parents the question that had been rolling round and round in his mind.

"What's a special education class anyway?" he asked.

Mom and Dad looked at each other a long time before he got an answer. It was like they were ready to draw straws to see who answered him. Neither of them seemed in much of a hurry to be the first. Finally his mom spoke.

"It's a special class. For children who are having learning problems."

All kinds of feelings mixed together inside Bobby. In a way he felt angry with Mrs. Roth and with his parents. Mrs. Roth had a nerve. She just wanted to get rid of him. And his parents were letting her do this to him. They just didn't want to bother coming up to school everytime she waved her pinky. In a way he felt put down. They were dumping him in a problem class. Bad or dumb, he was still a problem. Well he would show them. If he was a problem it would be because he gave them a hard time. Not because he was stupid. Yet in another way, Bobby felt as though it might not be such a terrible thing after all, putting him in this new class. Mom said it was for children who had learning problems. And he had a problem learning to read. Maybe Miss Martin was an extra special, smart teacher who could get him to read. Maybe that was why the class was special. Bobby didn't know. He got up and went to his room, without looking at or answering his parents.

Chapter Four

THE NEXT DAY Bobby woke up with his stomach hurting. He thought of staying home but then he figured he might as well go and get it over with. His stomach would hurt again tomorrow if he didn't go to school today. Maybe Miss Martin could help him. Maybe it was worth a try.

When he went to school he walked all around the back of the yard so that he wouldn't pass Mrs. Roth's line. He didn't want the kids to see him. They would wonder why he didn't join the line and they would notice where he was going. Bobby looked around for Miss Martin's line. He saw Mrs. Roth motioning to him, and pointing to a corner of the yard. Bobby walked slowly to the far corner.

He stood to the side looking around. A teacher walked up to him. "I'm Miss Martin," she said. "Are you Bobby Dawson?"

Bobby nodded. He looked at Miss Martin. She was short, with greyish brown hair, and she looked kind of nervous. So far, Bobby couldn't see anything special about her. "Our line is here," she said. She waved her hand. "Okay," she said. "Let's go children."

When Bobby got to the room he looked around. He felt like a visitor in a strange place. The feeling was strong within him that he was just visiting with this class for a short time. That when the time passed, he would return to Mrs. Roth's room where he really belonged.

At first Bobby stayed on the sidelines. He acted like a watching kind of visitor, drinking in the surroundings before he joined them. He stayed to see what was going on here, a stranger in a strange scene.

To Bobby, the scene was a weird one. There were only ten kids in the whole class. At first Bobby thought the other kids were late, or would come on a bus or something. But that was it, ten kids and no more. Probably, he figured, that was why the class was special. Miss Martin could give special attention to everyone if the class was so small.

Right off, Bobby noticed something different about the class. In Mrs. Roth's class you had to raise your hand before you spoke. Here, Miss Martin let the kids say anything they wanted. They just spoke right out.

They walked around the room whenever they felt like it, too. Mrs. Roth would have had a fit. There didn't seem to be any routine and nothing seemed to be organized. Except that everybody had a job to do.

"I'm the eraser," one kid told Bobby proudly. "Nobody but me erases the board."

Big deal, Bobby thought. The kid could keep his job and erase every blackboard in school for all he cared. A girl said, "I take care of the gerbils. Only me."

It seemed that having a job made these kids feel special and important. As though without having something all to themselves, something nobody else could do, they wouldn't be as good as other kids.

The work Miss Martin gave seemed weird too. Some of the work was too hard for most of the kids and other work was real baby stuff. Bobby felt annoyed at having to do the baby stuff. Sometimes when a kid couldn't do his work he would get upset. There was a kid named Tommy who crumpled up his paper and threw it across the room when he couldn't do the work. "Give me another paper," he would say. "This one's yukky."

Miss Martin yelled at Tommy a lot. Funny, Bobby never thought Miss Martin would yell. He thought she'd be patient, sit with one kid at a time, and talk softly. She got mad a lot though. Especially at a kid named Dan, who ran around the room all the time, yelling Indian war cries.

In Mrs. Roth's class if you didn't get the work right, Mrs. Roth would give you a low grade, and let you know she sure wasn't happy. But here, if the kids got something right they wanted Miss Martin to make a big fuss over them. She gave out all kinds of silly things, potato chips, candy, or gold stars, just like they were kindergarten babies.

Bobby had thought the kids were in Miss Martin's class because they had trouble reading, the way he did. But there seemed to be different things wrong with all the kids. A pretty girl named Marie never talked. She just sat, walked around sometimes, and never said one single word. A girl named Linda sat holding her knees and rocking half the time. Miss Martin gave her a pill a few times a day. Bobby felt bad for the other kids, but being in this class didn't seem to be doing them or him any good.

Miss Martin let Bobby sit and draw all he wanted. That was okay sometimes, but it didn't help him learn to read. How could you read if you sat drawing all the time? Bobby had hoped that Miss Martin would sit with him, and help him figure out letters, so he could learn to read like other nine year olds. But she acted nervous all the time and too busy for him. She was always either yelling at Tommy or chasing Dan around the room as he ran and whooped.

When Bobby complained to his parents they said things like, "you have to get adjusted," or, "give it a chance," or "it's too soon to tell how it will work out." But day after day Bobby sat in class feeling miserable. Nothing changed. Every day was the same. Bobby still

didn't feel a part of the group. He still felt like a visitor. But now, more and more, a visitor who wanted to go home, a visitor who couldn't stand the place for one more minute. Bobby was bored to death with sitting around drawing all the time. He was sick of Miss Martin's nervous yelling, and Dan's Indian war cries were driving him up a wall.

Each morning Bobby awoke, ate breakfast barely speaking to his family, and set out for school. Each morning Bobby tried to avoid the kids in his old class and sneak around to Miss Martin's line. And each morning he sat in class feeling the same way. He was a visitor, locked in and forced into a strange place, an unwilling visitor, unable to find his way out. It was like trying to awake from a nightmare when deep inside your head you knew you were dreaming. Miss Martin's class felt like a bad dream.

Bobby wore his football sweater every day. The warmth of it as the September days grew chill gave him a sense of protection. Bobby couldn't get his name to come out right when he wrote it, he couldn't get the words to come out right when he read them, and here in Miss Martin's class he was losing his sense of being Bobby Dawson. The sweater, with the number 10 written boldly across the front, said Bobby more clearly to him than any other written sign. The sweater, a symbol of a football player with a name so like his, kept him from pinching himself to be sure that he was awake. When Linda rocked, Marie sat silently and Dan's war cries pierced the quiet, Bobby fingered the plushness of his sweater. Then the nightmarish feeling lifted a little as the softness surrounding the number 10 told him that he was awake, and that he was really here, really Bobby.

Still day after day hanging on to himself grew harder. And then one afternoon at three there was a rapid dismissal. Usually Miss

Martin's class was dismissed ten minutes earlier than other classes in the school. Bobby could get away before the other kids came out, before they could see him, before they could look at him and read the shame on his face. But this day, a gong rang out, everyone left the school quickly as in a fire drill, and everyone was sent home at once.

Bobby looked around, saw nobody he knew, and walked around the schoolyard toward home. Kids were all over the place, going in all directions. Then through the denseness of kids and sounds Bobby heard an old familiar voice and the words of an old, long forgotten jingle:

> Kindergarten baby.
> Stick your head in gravy.
> Kindergarten baby.
> Stick your head in gravy.

It was Maurice's voice. Bobby would know that creep's voice anywhere. He looked around trying to find the fat mouth that went with the voice.

"Bobby, baby," the voice went on. "Think they'll ever let you out of the crazy kid's kindergarten?"

Then, through the crowds Bobby saw him. He was standing near the school yard railing, a little ways from the open gate. Bobby bent down, out of sight, and wove his way through the stream of kids still pouring out onto the sidewalk. He scooped up a pile of autumn leaves as he went. He could feel twigs and pebbles mixed in with the leaves.

Bobby got to the gate, ran inside the schoolyard quickly and quietly, and stood behind Maurice. Maurice still stood in the same

spot, right outside the fence, his back now turned to Bobby. Maurice looked straight ahead of him. "Where are you Bobby, baby?" he called. "Gone home to play with your blocks?"

Bobby reached through the schoolyard railing from behind. Using both his hands, he stuffed Maurice's big mouth with autumn leaves, mixed with the twigs, pebbles and all. Then pausing just long enough to enjoy the stunned look on Maurice's stuffed up face, he ran faster and faster away from school and toward home.

Bobby opened the front door and leaned against the inside, trying to catch his breath. "That you Bobby," Mrs. Allan called.

"It's me, Mrs. Allan," he said shakily. "I'm taking Sprint for a walk."

"Come on in and have a cookie, warm from the oven."

Bobby walked in, ate a chocolate chip cookie, and hugged Mrs. Allan.

"You were always so good to me Mrs. Allan," he said quietly.

"Why thank you Bobby," she said with a smile in her voice. "That was worth baking for."

There was no use in upsetting Mrs. Allan. She had always been good to him. And her food had always warmed him when he felt cold inside or out. There was no use in telling her that he had just about had it. That he belonged nowhere. Not at home, not at school. That Maurice's taunting had been the last straw. That now, he was taking Sprint and he was leaving, and that he would never be coming back.

Chapter Five

BOBBY LEFT the house with Sprint, for the last time. He didn't know where he would go, not yet, but he knew he had to get as far away from here as possible. Before he left, though, he wanted to see his Aunt Lillian again. She and Mrs. Allan were the only grownups who really cared about him, who always spoke softly to him, who made him feel wrapped in warmth, like his football sweater. Bobby knew that he had to take two buses to see Aunt Lillian. He and Annette had made the trip a few times in July, when school was out and his folks were at work.

The first bus stopped in front of the church two blocks away. Bobby walked there, waited, and stepped up when the bus pulled near the curb.

"You can't take that dog on the bus," the driver said gruffly.

"But I have to get to Aunt Lillian's," Bobby said.

"Sorry kid," the driver said. The door slammed, the bus pulled away, and Bobby and Sprint stood alone at the curb.

He should have thought of it. They didn't let dogs on buses. Bobby hadn't owned a dog long enough to know all the rules. He knew that he couldn't leave Sprint behind. But he had to have time to figure out where to go, and how to get there. A picture of the beach flashed through Bobby's mind. He could go there, and stay with Sprint until he thought out his next move. But how would he get to the beach?

Bobby remembered the last time he went to the beach, the day the Morrisons drove him there. He remembered Mr. Morrison pointing to the big sprawling house where Dr. Adamson lived. He

had made a note that the vet's house was four blocks from the beach. Bobby looked around. He saw a man and a woman strolling with a big, beautiful collie. He walked up to the couple.

"Excuse me," he said. "But my Sprint here isn't feeling too good. My folks told me to take him to Dr. Adamson, but I don't remember just where he lives."

"Oh, sure," the woman said. "We know Dr. Adamson. He's a great vet."

"Can you tell me how to get there?"

"Sure," the man answered. "Just turn here, and walk straight to Maple Street. It's a long walk, though. Nearly a mile."

"That's okay." Bobby said. "We like to walk."

Bobby walked straight, recognizing some of the stores and houses. He walked quickly and pretty soon he spotted the huge, sprawling old house with the sign on the lawn. He remembered that the vet was four blocks from the beach parking lot. He continued on, crossed the deserted lot and walked onto the beach.

He looked around. He and Sprint were alone on the beach. The happy, noisy crowds had vanished with the summer sun. Bobby ran with Sprint for awhile. When he sat on the sand, his back against the rocks that jutted out past the shoreline. He had to decide where to go. Maybe, he thought, maybe he could go out west. Maybe he could find Bobby Dryfuss. If he told Bobby Dryfuss how close he felt toward him, the quarterback might help him. He and Sprint could travel with the team. Sprint could be the mascot, and Bobby could help out all kinds of ways. But how could he get out west? Hitch? How many people would pick up a boy and a dog without asking a whole lot of questions?

Bobby stayed on the beach for a long time. Briefly, the thought of home flitted past his mind. Then he pushed it away. He didn't want to go home, even if he was wanted there. In a way, he didn't blame everybody for not wanting him. In a way he blamed himself. He had let everybody down, been a disappointment to his family, a son who was too dumb to learn how to read.

It would never be any good. If he went home he'd get shoved back into Miss Martin's class. The other kids would make fun of him. Not only Maurice, but pretty soon, Charlie and Steve, and the kids who mattered. He would be a freak in everyone's eyes.

Bobby looked up at the sky. The sun was starting to move farther out toward the horizon. By now his folks would be home. By now they would start to wonder what had happened to him. Let them, Bobby thought. He didn't care about how worried they got. They were the ones who let him get shoved into that class.

Bobby ran with Sprint awhile to keep warm, then he sat back on the rocks. He drew his sweater tight around him, and hugged Sprint. The dog was starting to shiver. Bobby sat, the chill and hunger setting in as the sun began to disappear into the greying water, and the evening tide rose higher near the shore.

"Hey," a voice called, "Hey, come here. There they are. The dog and the kid with the football sweater."

Bobby turned and saw the blue uniform through the light of the still setting sun. He got up and began to run. Then two arms reached behind him and knocked him gently to the soft sand.

"You've got a great offense there kid," the policeman said quietly. "But I'm a pretty good tackle." He sat down on the sand, next to Bobby, not even worrying about his neat blue uniform. Bobby turned, the policeman's arms still around him. He leaned against the policeman's chest and let the tears come, as the strong arms rocked him gently to the rhythm of the ocean's waves.

Bobby sat in the squad car between two police officers. He leaned

close to the officer who had found him, who had held him as he wept. There was something about the policeman, whose name he didn't even know, that reminded him of his father. Not the way he looked but the feel of him. The feel of his strong arms, of his chest as Bobby's head leaned against it. It was like the old days with Dad. The loving days when it was still okay to be hurt and be comforted, when he was still young enough to make being babyish all right. Before he had to be grown up and live up to the number that told his age.

When the squad car pulled up Sprint ran from the back seat, barking and leading the way. Bobby stood outside, lingering, the urge to leave again forming in his mind. Then his family was running toward him. In a second three pairs of arms were around him, holding him, hugging him. His Mom, Dad, and Annette were all around him, closing him inside a circle of warmth and caring, right outside in the middle of the street, where anyone could see. Everyone began talking at once.

"We were so worried."

"You don't know how wonderful it is to see you."

"You're home safe. That's all that matters."

"Thank you officers. Thank you for finding our Bobby."

When the policemen left, the family went into the house, still enfolding Bobby.

"Mrs. Allan called me at the library," Mom said. "And asked me to come home right away. She started to worry when you didn't come back with Sprint after awhile. Then Maurice's mother phoned the house and told her what happened. Mrs. Allan thought of the way you said goodbye to her before you went out. She put two and two together and got terribly upset."

"We all came home and after awhile we went to look for you,"

Dad said. "We drove all around and when we couldn't find you we called the police. They found a bus driver who remembered a boy trying to board the bus with a dog. The boy said he had to get to Aunt Lillian. But you weren't at her house either."

Bobby looked at his folks. They really did seem to care. They had been terribly worried about him. And they were relieved and happy to have him home safe and sound. But what had changed? He was back in the book filled house he had tried to escape, and Miss Martin's special education class still awaited him with the morning light.

"It's no good," he said clearly. "Bringing me home won't help. I still can't go back to that class. And I still can't read like the other kids."

"I'll help you Bobby," Annette said.

She put her arm around her brother's neck. "I'll work with you every single day after school. For as long as it takes."

Bobby took Annette's hand. "Thanks sis," he said softly. "But you're still a kid. It would take more than you helping to get me to read."

"Bobby's right," Dad said. "We haven't solved anything. Not yet anyway."

"But we will," Mom said. "We'll work hard at finding out what's wrong. And when we do we'll work twice as hard getting it taken care of."

The door opened. "Bobby never came," Aunt Lillian's voice called frantically. "I couldn't wait any longer. I left a neighbor in my house in case he turned up and I rushed here." She walked into the living room. "Oh Bobby," she cried, hugging him. "I was never so happy to see anyone in my whole life."

Aunt Lillian kept hugging him and hugging him as though she

would never let him go. But Bobby didn't mind. Aunt Lillian's hug had a never changing soft coziness about it. It was a hug you could count on.

"They told me you tried to get on the bus with Sprint. That you were coming to see me. I waited and waited."

"We're so sorry Lil," Mom said. "We should have called you the second Bobby came home. But we were just so excited."

"I understand. I would have been on my way here by then anyway. But Bobby's home now and that's all that matters. Everything's okay."

"No. It's not," Mom said. "We were just talking. And we have to get to the bottom of this. Of what's bothering Bobby, why he doesn't read well."

"How will you do that?" Aunt Lillian asked.

"We'll see people. Ask questions. Do research." Dad said. "An editor and a librarian ought to be able to handle the job."

"Will I have to go back to Miss Martin's class?" Bobby asked.

His parents looked at each other.

"No," Dad said. "You can take a little vacation while we all try to find out what's best."

"Then can I stay at Aunt Lillian's," Bobby asked excitedly. "For a few days?"

"If it's okay with Aunt Lillian. We will be busy for a few day making calls."

"You bet it's okay," Aunt Lillian said. "I haven't had a child around since Lucy went off to college. You can move in anytime."

"Sprint too?" Bobby asked.

Aunt Lillian laughed, "Sprint too. If you walk him and bring his food."

"Sure Aunt Lillian." Bobby turned to his folks. "Can I go home with Aunt Lillian?"

"After we all have dinner together," Mom said. "But just for a few days. Just till we do some research. Then you'll come home. And whatever is wrong, we'll face it together."

Chapter Six

THE TIME at Aunt Lillian's house was like a vacation. A time of hugs, and walks, and warm, cozy dinners. A time away from pressures and problems. Then one night Mom and Dad came over to Aunt Lil's house.

"I think we may be on the right track," Mom said excitedly. "About what your problem is. I found a book in the library. It's called *Can't Read and Write Right,* by a man who had the same kind of trouble."

"Well what is it?" Bobby asked. "What's the matter with me?"

"Let's wait and see before we say anything for sure," Dad said. "We've made an appointment with Dr. Corman at the testing lab for tomorrow."

"What's wrong with Dr. Ried? We always see him when there's anything the matter with us."

Mom laughed, "Dr. Corman is a different kind of doctor. He works in schools and he tests youngsters who have trouble learning, so he can find out what's wrong."

"I never heard of a doctor like that," Bobby said. "But I sure hope it works."

The Dawsons took Bobby home after dinner at Aunt Lil's and the next day Bobby sat in Dr. Corman's office. Dr. Corman didn't wear a white coat or a stethoscope around his neck. He had all kinds of school stuff in his office. Bobby had never seen this kind of doctor's office before.

For two days Bobby took all kinds of tests. He read, he wrote, he answered questions, built with blocks, solved puzzles and problems.

He was beginning to feel like the guinea pig in Mrs. Roth's Science corner.

Then after going over the tests, Dr. Corman called the Dawsons into his office.

"It's what you suspected Mrs. Dawson," he said. Then he turned to Bobby. "Bobby," he said. "You have dyslexia."

"Dyslexia," Bobby said. "What kind of disease is that? And how come it lasts so long? Even when I had chicken pox real bad it didn't last this long."

Dr. Corman threw back his head and laughed heartily. It was a good, friendly, warm laugh and it made Bobby like Dr. Corman. "It's not a disease like chicken pox, Bobby. It's a learning problem. And it's pretty common. We don't know just what causes it. But it's a condition that gives a youngster trouble focusing on symbols on a printed page. It has nothing to do with how smart you are. In fact the tests show that you have very high intelligence. You're a very bright boy."

"I know. I could have told you that," Bobby said.

Dr. Corman threw back his head and laughed again. "I guess you could have at that, Bobby, and here I bothered to take all those tests."

Bobby laughed. "Well now that we know about this dyslexia thing Dr. Corman, how do we cure it?"

"We don't exactly cure it Bobby," Dr. Corman answered. "We deal with it, overcome it, learn to read in spite of it."

"How? I tried very hard."

"I know but never in the right way before. You need special help and I mean special. Not like the class you told me about. You need to be taught in a school where people understand the problem and where there is a large staff of people to help all the children."

"But where will we find a school like that?" Bobby asked.

"I'm recommending you to the Einstein school," Dr. Corman said. "It's a great place and I think it's perfect for you." He turned to Mr. and Mrs. Dawson. "It's a private school. You pay according to your means. And there's a fund given by the state. Is that okay with you?"

The Dawsons nodded. "If it's best for Bobby, sure it's okay," Mrs. Dawson said.

"Good." Dr. Corman turned to Bobby. "Do you know why it's called the Einstein school?" he asked.

Bobby shook his head. "No. Why?"

"It's named for Albert Einstein. It's believed that he had dyslexia too. And so did Thomas Edison, and Woodrow Wilson, Winston Churchill, and Nelson Rockefeller and General Patton and many, many others."

"No kidding," Bobby said proudly. "Einstein, Edison, Wilson, Churchill, Patton, Rocky and me."

The Einstein school sure was something special. Bobby spent part of his first day taking in everything. There were no more than ten kids in each class and there were grownups all over the place. There were teachers, and people who helped the teachers by tutoring the kids one at a time. There were college students who were learning to be teachers. They helped too. Dr. Corman was around part of the time also. Bobby noticed that most of the kids were boys. He asked Dr. Corman about it.

"We don't know why Bobby," Dr. Corman said. "But three of every four children who have dyslexia are boys."

The Einstein school was really spacious. There were loads of rooms to do your work. There were corners with tables or mats where you could read privately or with tutors. There were books, games, paper, crayons and everything was set up to look homelike and comfortable. After Bobby had a chance to look around he met his teacher.

A cool looking young guy with long blonde hair, wearing jeans and a t-shirt walked up to him.

"Hi there," he said. He studied Bobby's sweater. "Let's see," he said. "Bet I can guess your name. It's Bobby, right?"

Bobby nodded. "That's right."

"I read it on your football sweater. 10 for Bobby Dryfuss of the Western Stars."

Bobby laughed. "You read football sweaters?" he said.

"Sure and so do you it seems. But before we're through you'll be reading books instead of sweaters. I'm John Cooper, your teacher."

"You're my teacher?" Bobby said in a surprised voice.

"Sure am. And you're going to learn too. So let's get it on the road."

Mr. Cooper was only one of the people who helped Bobby. Sometimes he worked in a small group with Mrs. Samuel, and sometimes he worked with a college student named Joann. Everybody got a lot of attention, but sometimes the more attention you got, the more you wanted. At first Bobby would interrupt at group time, saying "it's my turn" or "I asked a question," or "I need help now." The teachers were very understanding, and after awhile Bobby learned to have more patience.

The great thing about the Einstein school was that nobody had to fake it. Everybody knew why they were there. When you all had the same problem there was no need to hide it. Lots of the books were made in a special way, with large pictures next to the words. The words were printed in large type, to make it easier to figure them out. And the teachers sat with you dividing up words, going over and over the sounds that made up each word.

Mr. Cooper was terrific. Bobby liked him more than any other teacher he'd ever known. When you needed help Mr. Cooper was there. He taught the class as a whole sometimes, and at other times he helped with groups and private tutoring. Bobby worked very, very hard, trying his best. Yet he still couldn't quite make it. He still couldn't really read. It was like climbing a mountain, using his feet and hands, going, up, up, up, almost but not quite reaching the peak. Mr. Cooper said it was just a matter of patience and work and it would come.

They didn't work all the time though. There were sports—football, volleyball—and there was music. Mr. Cooper loved to play the guitar and he was great at it. Bobby told him he could quit teaching and work in a rock group, but Mr. Cooper laughed and said he was a teacher and that's what he loved doing best in the whole world.

Mr. Cooper called the class around him. They would sit in a circle, on the floor, while Mr. Cooper sat on a stool, strumming his guitar. They would sing all kinds of songs together as Mr. Cooper played. Sometimes Mr. Cooper gave out sheets of paper, with notes and

words on them, so that the children could see the printed words of the songs they were singing. Those who had begun to read could follow along, while the others tried.

Then one morning Mr. Cooper called the class around him. He gave out song sheets and they were going to have a folk song festival. He played an old Scottish folk song called "Aiken Drum." Everyone sang the chorus after him:

> There was a man lived in the moon,
> Lived in the moon,
> There was a man lived in the moon,
> And his name was Aiken Drum.

There were some funny verses, like:

> His head was made of green cheese,
> Green cheese, green cheese, green cheese,
> His head was made of green cheese
> And his name was Aiken Drum.

Then Mr. Cooper gave out more song sheets and said they were going to learn another folk song using a person's name.

The song was called "Jennie Jenkins."

Mr. Cooper strummed and sang:

> Will you wear red, oh my dear, oh my dear,
> Will you wear read, Jennie Jenkins?
> No I won't wear red,
> It's the color of my head.
> Roll, Jennie Jenkins, roll.

Everybody snapped their fingers and sang the lines to the verse along with him. Then Mr. Cooper told the class to look at the next verse. Bobby looked at it too. Frankie Reynolds laughed as Mr. Cooper sang. He used Frankie's name instead of Jennie Jenkins and changed the song around. The kids tried to follow the song sheet as Mr. Cooper went on with:

Will you wear yellow, oh my dear, oh my dear,
Will you wear yellow, Frankie Reynolds?
No I won't wear yellow. It's the color of jello.
Roll, Frankie Reynolds, roll.

Everyone laughed and sang, "roll, Frankie Reynolds, roll."

Mr. Cooper asked the class to study the third verse for awhile. He strummed his guitar and sang the first line softly. "Will you wear green, oh my dear, oh my dear." He strummed for a few minutes more as the class looked at the song sheet. Then suddenly, all at once, as Bobby stared at the page, the funny squiggles he had seen all his life turned into letters, real letters, and the letters came together and made words. Bobby took a deep breath and sang out clearly as Mr. Cooper strummed:

Will you wear green, Bobby Dawson?
No I won't wear green.
It's the color of a bean.
Roll, Bobby Dawson, roll.

It was his name, and he had read it. He had read the whole verse. He had climbed all the way up. He had reached the peak. And now he stood high on top of the mountain.

"Hey wow. Hey everybody. I did it," he yelled out proudly.

The class clapped for him. Then they all joined in, Mr. Cooper playing his guitar, and Bobby leading the singing. They sang together, clearly and happily:

> Will you wear green, oh my dear, oh my dear.
> Will you wear green, Bobby Dawson?
> No I won't wear green.
> It's the color of a bean.
> Roll, Bobby Dawson, roll.
> Roll, Bobby Dawson, roll.